REAL WORLD ECONOMICS™

How Buying and Selling Futures Work

Susan Meyer

ROSEN
PUBLISHING®

New York

To Terry Meyer

Published in 2011 by The Rosen Publishing Group, Inc.
29 East 21st Street, New York, NY 10010

Copyright © 2011 by The Rosen Publishing Group, Inc.

First Edition

Library of Congress Cataloging-in-Publication Data

Meyer, Susan, 1986–
How buying and selling futures work / Susan Meyer.
    p. cm.—(Real world economics)
Includes bibliographical references and index.
ISBN 978-1-4488-1275-2 (library binding)
1. Futures market—United States—Juvenile literature. 2. Commodity futures—United States—Juvenile literature. 3. Futures—United States—Juvenile literature. 4. Commodity exchanges—United States—Juvenile literature. I. Title.
HG6024.M49 2011
332.64'52—dc22

                                                                    2010011321

Manufactured in the United States of America

CPSIA Compliance Information: Batch #W11YA: For further information, contact Rosen Publishing, New York, New York, at 1-800-237-9932.

On the cover: Traders signal offers to buy and sell futures contracts at the Standard & Poor's 500 stock index futures pit of the CME Group, the world's largest futures and options exchange, in Chicago, Illinois.

Contents

INTRODUCTION

Every morning when we wake up, we probably have a glass of orange juice and some toast or cereal for breakfast. Then we might get in a car or bus to ride to school. But we rarely stop to wonder where the gasoline in the car or bus, or the wheat in our cereal or toast, comes from. These things—oranges, wheat, oil for gasoline—are all commodities. A commodity is a raw, unprocessed good.

Some people make—or lose—a lot of money on commodities by betting on how much they will be worth at a certain point in the future. These people buy and sell contracts based on whether they think there will be more or less of the commodity available in the near future. If the supply of the commodity is large, prices for it will be lower. If the supply is small, prices will rise. The trick for a futures trader is to guess correctly what the availability and resulting price will be for a given commodity. In one of these contracts, a person must promise to buy or

sell a certain amount of a commodity at a certain price to be delivered on a certain date. These contracts are called futures contracts or, sometimes, simply futures. A contract is a legally binding agreement.

Here's an easy way to think of it: imagine Sean has an Aunt Pat who grows delicious tomatoes in her greenhouse. Aunt Pat tells Sean she's going to sell her tomatoes at the local farmer's market. Sean loves Aunt Pat's tomatoes, and he wants to make sure she saves some for him. So Sean calls her up before the farmer's market and asks her if she'll save him 5 pounds (2.3 kilograms) of tomatoes. In return, Sean promises her that he will buy those five pounds of tomatoes at $2 a pound (.45 kg).

When Sean gets to the farmer's market, Aunt Pat is having a really good day. Because the weather has been unseasonably cold, the local growers, who didn't have the benefit of Aunt Pat's wonderful greenhouse, didn't raise a very good crop of

These oranges are being harvested in Florida, the second largest producer of oranges in the world. Oranges are one of the major commodities for Florida.

tomatoes. Since Aunt Pat is the only one at the market with a good supply of juicy tomatoes, she is able to sell them for $3 a pound. But because she had already promised Sean some at $2 a pound, he is able to save some money. She, on the other hand, loses $5 in selling to Sean at the previously agreed-upon price. She could have sold those five pounds of tomatoes to the general public at the farmer's market for $15, not $10.

However, the situation could have easily been reversed. Imagine now that when Sean gets to the market, Aunt Pat and her tomatoes are not having such a good day. Because it has been so sunny and warm this summer, all the local growers have brought large crops of tomatoes to the market. There are so many tomatoes there that Aunt Pat is practically giving hers away at only $1 a pound. Because Sean promised Aunt Pat that he would buy them at $2 a pound, he is now actually paying twice as much as any other tomato buyer that day. Basically, by setting a promised price with Aunt Pat in advance, Sean was making a bet on how much he thought the tomatoes would be worth. He might not have known it, but Sean was entering into an informal futures contract.

Futures contracts can change in value very quickly because of changes in weather, politics, or commodity experts' best guesses as to what will happen in the coming weeks and months. For this reason, futures contracts are considered a risky investment. There is a possibility of earning a lot of money very quickly, but it is just as easy to lose a lot of money very quickly.

CHAPTER ONE

WHAT ARE FUTURES MARKETS AND WHO ARE THE MAIN PLAYERS?

Chicago, Illinois, in the 1840s was an exciting place to be. It was quickly becoming a bustling center of commerce for the United States. Chicago's central location in the American heartland made it a great place for railroads carrying goods and commodities to stop. Chicago also offered access to the waterways of the Great Lakes, making it easy to reach the city by commercial boats. Because of these factors, Chicago was quickly becoming a major transportation and distribution hub for the entire country. This was especially true of agricultural commodities—such as wheat, corn, and livestock—that would be funneled from the farms and ranches of the West and Midwest to the markets of the East.

THE CHICAGO BOARD OF TRADE

Farmers all over the Midwest would bring their harvested grain to Chicago to sell to merchants there. This was a good

In the early 1860s, Chicago, seen here, was a bustling center of commerce, in large part because of its extensive commercial waterways.

system except for one thing: when all of the farmers brought their grain to market at the same time, Chicago was filled with more grain than it could sell or even store. This was bad for the farmers because the price of grain went down when there was so much of it available. Another problem was the lack of storage for excess grain. There are stories of farmers dumping their grain into the Chicago River because prices were too low to sell it, and they couldn't afford to haul it to another city to sell.

To address these problems and keep the river free of dumped grain, a group of local businessmen formed an organization called the Chicago Board of Trade (CBOT) in 1848. The CBOT created arrangements that were known as to-arrive contracts. These to-arrive contracts would later evolve into futures contracts. Basically, to-arrive contracts allowed farmers to sell their grain before delivering it. Farmers could harvest their grain and then enter into a contract to sell it at a promised price and deliver it on a certain date. Then the farmers could hold the grain at a storage facility outside of Chicago and agree to deliver to an agreed-upon location on the date specified in the contract.

The Sometimes Disastrous Past of Chicago's Futures Markets

Chicago continues to be an important center of the futures market. Unfortunately, things have not always gone smoothly for the city or its market. In 1871, the Great Chicago Fire destroyed a large part of the city's financial district, including six of the seventeen grain storage units that were used as delivery points for futures contracts. The CBOT headquarters was also burned to the ground, and many important records were lost.

Disaster struck again in 1992. This time, instead of a fire, Chicago was hit by a flood. The Great Chicago Flood began when some transit workers accidentally caused water from the Chicago River to flood a railway tunnel. Water was soon pouring through a maze of tunnels under the city's streets. The CBOT had to halt all operations as water flowed into the basement of its headquarters. The flooding caused power outages and the evacuation of all of downtown Chicago. It was an extremely costly business disaster because the financial district was the most affected part of the city. It was not only a loss for Chicago financial markets, however. National and global markets were also negatively affected when Chicago temporarily closed its futures market. When markets are closed, trades aren't being made, business isn't being conducted, and no one is making any money.

To-Arrive Contracts

To-arrive contracts were beneficial for both the farmers growing the grain and the merchants buying the grain. Let's return to the example of Aunt Pat and her tomatoes. Sean asked his Aunt Pat to save him some tomatoes at $2 a pound (.45 kg) before he knew how much they would sell for at the farmer's market. Now suppose that Sean didn't just enjoy eating Aunt Pat's tomatoes, but he also used them in his own business.

Sean needed fresh tomatoes to make his famous tomato soup, which is sold at his popular local restaurant. In a sense, Aunt Pat is the farmer, and Sean is the merchant. By getting a certain price and quantity of tomatoes promised to him in advance, Sean guarantees that he will have enough to make his soup. Also, Sean knows exactly what the cost of the tomatoes will be, so he can budget for the expense in advance. So even if Sean ends up paying more for Aunt Pat's tomatoes than he would have if he'd bought them on the open market, at least he knows ahead of time that he can definitely put his soup on the menu. He has secured a guaranteed source of tomatoes at a guaranteed price that he has budgeted for.

This situation is also advantageous to Aunt Pat. Although she might not know the price she will be able to get for the rest of her tomatoes, or how many she'll be able to sell to other buyers, she can at least know in advance that she is sure to sell 5 pounds (2.3 kg) at a guaranteed price. With Sean's tomato order and promised price, she knows she won't have to cart all of her tomatoes home without making a sale. The farmer wins, and the merchant wins. Everyone seems to get what they want in this version of the futures market.

These pit traders are using a system of hand signals to communicate trades of futures contracts at the Chicago Mercantile Exchange.

13

Pit Traders

Futures are usually traded in pits on trading exchange floors. These pits are octagonal (eight-sided) areas of a trading floor in which the people trading futures contracts stand. The only people allowed in trading pits are people who are part of a recognized futures trading organization. The actual trading of the contracts is a very loud and exciting business. Traders stand in the pit and shout out their orders. They shout what prices they are willing to pay or accept. Often, they also use hand signals to communicate their bids and offers to people who might not be able to hear them because of all the noise. The transactions are made simply by traders agreeing on a price and the number of contracts to trade. Most pit traders are very young due to the stress and physical demands of the job.

Electronic Trading

In recent years, some trading has moved from the pit floor to electronic trading terminals. Electronic screen-based trading works much the same way as pit trading does. All traders must be members of a recognized futures exchange in order to trade futures electronically. In electronic trading, buyers enter

Traders working in a futures pit, such as this one at the New York Mercantile Exchange, can observe changes in futures prices entered electronically and displayed on screens.

their bids and offers into a computer system. The computer system then displays this information and allows sellers to agree to the trade electronically.

In the United States, pit trading is still more common than electronic trading because of its long history and tradition. Traders who trade on the floor in pits have long resisted electronic trading. The United States is the only country where both pit trading and electronic trading are commonly used. In other countries, electronic trading is beginning to make pit trading obsolete. In the future, electronic screen-based trading may become more widely used in the United States.

Futures Traders and Brokers

Trading pits and electronic terminals have one thing in common: Regardless of whether the futures trading is done on the floor of the exchange or over the Internet, the people doing the actual trading must be employed by a futures exchange. A futures exchange is a corporation with members. Each of the members pays for a place within the futures exchange. Their memberships are more commonly called seats. The members of the exchange are the only ones allowed to execute transactions on the exchange. These members fall into one of two groups: floor traders and brokers.

The floor traders, sometimes called locals, are the ones standing in the pits or at the electronic terminals actually making the trades. They have different styles of trading but usually fall into one of three categories. A scalper is a trader who buys or sells futures contracts and holds them for only a short period of time. Scalpers hope to profit quickly by buying contracts whose value they think will change quickly. The second type of floor trader is a day trader. A day trader holds a position open longer than a scalper, but still closes it out before the end of the day. Finally, there is the position trader. The position trader holds his or her position in the futures contract overnight. Day traders and position traders are very different from scalpers. They attempt to profit from the direction the market is going in and what they think will happen with commodity supplies and prices. Scalpers make many trades in the futures market each day for a slight profit. They make money from the difference in the bid price (the price offered to buy a contract) and the ask price (the price offered to sell a contract), also known as the bid-ask spread.

A broker is a person who makes trades for people who aren't members of the futures exchange. Anyone who wants to trade futures contracts but doesn't want or isn't able to join a futures exchange would have to go through a broker. In order to make money, a broker charges fees for trades that he or she makes.

SPECULATORS AND HEDGERS

Of course, not everyone can win in the futures market. Futures contracts were first devised in Chicago. They were primarily deals struck between the farmers who produced the commodity (such as grain) and the merchants who needed the commodity (such as suppliers for mills, which require grain to make flour). However, other people soon started to see that there was a chance to make money by trading futures contracts. These people, called speculators, have no direct interest in the commodity being traded but use the price changes in the market to make some money. Speculators hope to make money by buying an asset (something of value) at one price and then selling it at a higher price.

Kellogg's is the world's largest producer of cereal. The price it pays for grain commodities, such as wheat and rice, determines how much consumers pay for a box of cereal.

Returning to the example of Aunt Pat and her tomatoes, imagine that Sean has a cousin Pete who also asks Aunt Pat to set aside 5 pounds (2.3 kg) of tomatoes for him at $2 a pound (.45 kg). However, unlike Sean, Pete has no real need for five pounds of tomatoes. Pete might not even like tomatoes. Pete only wants Aunt Pat to set aside the five pounds of tomatoes for him because he has noticed this summer's unusually cold weather. He thinks there won't be very many tomatoes this season, and what little there are will sell at a high price. If he is right and Aunt Pat's tomatoes are worth $3 a pound instead of the $2 a pound he got them for, he can turn around and resell them for a profit.

Pete stands a chance of making some easy money. If he is wrong and the weather becomes nice before the end of the growing season, the market might be full of tomatoes. If this is the case, and Aunt Pat's tomatoes are only worth $1 a pound, Pete will end up losing money. Cousin Pete, as a speculator, takes on a big risk by making this investment.

He could make some quick money without much effort, or he could lose a lot of money very quickly.

Pete would be considered a speculator because he has no interest in the commodity itself (in this case, tomatoes). His business doesn't rely on it. Instead, he bought the tomatoes at one price and hoped to sell them in the future at a higher price to make money. Speculators will almost never actually receive a shipment of the commodity. Usually, they will trade the contract away before it comes time to actually buy and receive the commodity. The other players in the futures market are those who have a real interest in the commodity. These people are called hedgers. Hedgers might include millers who will make flour from wheat, or companies that package and sell frozen orange juice concentrate. Sean, in the above example with Aunt Pat, would be a hedger because he needs the tomatoes for his restaurant business.

CHAPTER TWO

WHAT ARE FUTURES CONTRACTS AND HOW DO THEY WORK?

A futures contract is the obligation to buy or sell something at a specific price at a specific time in the future. This can seem scary when someone is buying futures contracts for a product that he or she doesn't really want to use, as speculators do. Futures contracts usually represent huge quantities of a commodity. These huge quantities also usually cost a great deal. Even the biggest orange juice fans probably don't want several hundred pounds of oranges on their hands. Also, few orange juice drinkers can afford to pay for a lifetime supply of oranges all at once. Speculators might not actually want to end up with the commodity they are agreeing to purchase. The idea of an "obligation to buy" a commodity doesn't seem like a good idea.

OFFSETTING

Speculators don't actually want anyone showing up at their door to deliver the 100 pounds (45 kg) of oranges or five hundred squealing pigs they've agreed to purchase. That's why nearly all

Most traders offset futures contracts before delivery, so they never receive difficult-to-store and transport commodities such as live pigs.

speculators do something called offsetting. Offsetting means taking the opposite position in the contract in order to balance it. The opposite of buying is selling. The same is true of promising to buy. If a trader has a futures contract that says

he or she promises to buy 100 pounds of oranges, the trader can offset that contract by promising to sell 100 pounds of oranges. The opposite also holds true. A trader may enter a contract in which he or she promises to sell 100 pounds of oranges. The trader might not have 100 pounds of oranges to sell. In that case, the trader should offset his or her contract by entering another contract promising to buy 100 pounds of oranges. The two contracts cancel each other out.

It helps to think about it in this way: Susan really wants to buy a CD that her friend Matt has. She offers to pay Matt $10 for it. However, when it comes time to give him the money, Susan realizes that she can't afford it. Instead, she asks another friend if he wants to buy the CD. If the second friend agrees, he can give Susan $10 and she can give him the CD. Susan isn't out any money, and she has honored her agreement with Matt. In this case, the buying and selling of an item cancel each other out. This illustrates how the "obligation" to buy a commodity when one enters a futures contract isn't really that relevant. When buyers don't want to receive the commodity they've signed a purchase agreement for, they don't have to. All they have to do is offset their position by finding another buyer for the commodity who will take it off their hands. The reverse is also true. If Susan had promised Matt to sell him a CD that she didn't have, she could offset that obligation by finding someone else to sell it to her and then reselling it to Matt. Traders are able to promise to sell commodities they don't actually have possession of because they can always offset their position.

The Long and Short of Opening and Closing

The world of futures contracts has its own special terms. For example, when a person enters into a futures contract, he or she is said to be "opening a position." The position a person takes in a futures contract is not called buyer or seller, although that is basically what that person is.

When someone enters into a futures contract, he or she takes

24

one of two positions: the long position or the short position. The long position means the person is the buyer in the contract. A person taking the long position agrees to buy the commodity when the contract comes to its end at the price agreed upon.

This electronic screen displays the quickly changing prices of futures contracts for wheat. Traders can quickly digest the information displayed here and use it to make decisions.

The short position means the person is the seller in the contract. A person taking the short position in the contract agrees to sell the commodity when the contract comes to its end at the agreed-upon price.

A person who enters the contract in the long position (the buyer) "closes out" the position by offsetting it. Closing out means the holder of the contract doesn't have the contract anymore. To close out the position, the holder of the long position of a futures contract simply goes back into the market and offers the identical contract for sale.

Here's where the chance to gain or lose money in the futures market comes in. If the value of the commodity has gone down by the time the person with the long position closes out (sells off) the contract, that person loses the amount of money that the price went down. Of course, the reverse holds true if the value of the commodity has gone up. The person then earns money in the amount that the commodity's price went up. In the rare case that the person in the long position doesn't offset his or her position and close it out (sell it to someone else) by the time the contract expires, he or she owes the full price of the commodity originally agreed to in the contract.

In contrast to the person in the long position, the person in the short position (the seller) wants the value of the commodity to go up. If the value goes up, the person in the short position receives the difference when he or she closes the account. If the value drops, the person in the short position loses that amount of money. If the person in the short position doesn't offset his or her position, he or she must then sell the actual commodity (not just a contract for it) at the price agreed on in the contract. Again, this is extremely rare. Most people trading on the futures market don't have the actual commodity to sell. Futures contracts are usually closed out and sold to the actual people who want the commodities (like food processors) by the time the commodity's delivery date—and the contract's expiration—has arrived.

When Is a Commodity Not a Commodity?

It seems like a commodity can be almost anything that is grown, eaten, harvested, mined, or raised. But there is one notable and curious exception: onions. Under the federal laws governing futures markets in the United States, it is illegal to trade futures in onions. Onion futures were traded between 1942 and 1959 in the United States, but onion growers became concerned about falling prices. They blamed speculators and futures traders for their crop's loss in value. In response to the concerns of onion growers, the U.S. Congress prohibited dealings in onion futures in 1958.

As a result of this act, onions were excluded from the definition of commodities. If a futures exchange were to offer futures contracts in onions, traders who lost money could walk away without owing any of their debt because the contract would not have been legal in the first place. There are also financial penalties for anyone who trades onion futures. While not expressly stated as illegal in the statute, to this day no futures exchange has tried its luck with the onion's close relatives shallots, scallions, or leeks.

FINANCIAL FUTURES

Futures contracts started out as a way for buyers and sellers of commodities to avoid risk. The risks included crop failures and scarcity, bumper crops and oversupply, price spikes, and price collapses. Futures trading that is based on commodities is usually what people think of when they think about futures contracts. However, there is actually a whole other group of futures contracts. Futures are generally divided into two main groups: commodity futures and financial futures. Commodity futures cover most of the things we use every day—not only the wheat in our toast and the oranges used for juice, but also the wood and metal that make our houses, schools, and office buildings. Basically anything that is grown and harvested, mined from the earth, or raised as livestock is a commodity. Some of the most common commodity futures are corn, soybeans, oats, cattle, milk, lumber, cocoa, coffee, gold, orange juice, and oil.

For most of the history of futures trading, commodities futures were the only kind of futures contracts available. Futures markets were understood to apply only to things that could be tasted, grown, harvested, mined, extracted, delivered,

Raw lumber is a commodity that can be processed and used to make furniture, paper, and other goods. The prices of these manufactured items will all depend on the quantity of raw lumber available.

or consumed. This all changed in 1972, when people started to buy futures contracts on money itself. These futures, called currency futures, were based not on the change in value of commodities, but on the changing value of money. The value

People trade currency futures based on the changing value of international currencies. The value can change for any reason from natural disasters to war.

of money changes from day to day, just like the value of commodities does. While it may be strange to think about how a dollar might be worth more today than it is tomorrow, this is very often the case.

Many countries have different currencies, and the value of their currency can go up or down depending on what is going on in the national and global economies. The United States' currency is, of course, the dollar. The value of the dollar can go up or down in relation to the currencies of other countries. We call this the exchange rate. People who want to buy currency futures make bets on whether they think the value of the dollar will go up or down. They can also make bets on the exchange rates for different currencies from around the world, such as the Mexican peso or the British pound. Just as with commodity futures, if the value of money covered in the contract goes up, the seller of the contract earns money. However, if the value of the money covered in the contract goes down, the seller of the contract loses money.

31

Currency futures are only a small part of the separate category of financial futures. Financial futures include stocks, bonds, and currencies. Another type of financial future is based on the stock market. People can buy or sell futures contracts on stocks based on their belief that the stock market, the fortunes of particular industries, or the performance of individual companies will go up or down. Although commodity futures are still what people tend to primarily associate with futures markets, financial futures now account for approximately 75 percent of all futures contracts.

CHAPTER THREE
THE MARGINS THAT ARE CENTRAL TO FUTURES TRADING

The term "margin" is often heard in reference to the stock market. Buying on margin in the stock market basically means taking out a loan. When stocks are bought on margin, it means the purchaser puts down only some of the money that the stock is worth. But like most loans, this money must eventually be repaid with interest.

When talking about futures contracts, however, margin has a somewhat different meaning. In the futures market, the word "margin" means the amount of money that a person puts down in order to hold a futures contract. The initial margin requirement is the minimum amount of money the person has to put down in order to open the contract. However, unlike margin purchases in the stock market, the rest of the money owed on the purchase price of the contract is not borrowed. Since futures contracts are about buying a commodity, the margin is a down payment pending the eventual purchase (or sale) of the commodity. By putting down a little bit of money now, the person is agreeing to pay the remainder owed by either selling the contract to someone else (closing it out) or selling the actual commodity covered in the contract once it is delivered. The margin payment helps make sure that the person can handle the full financial obligation of the contract.

CLEARINGHOUSES

But who decides how much money the initial margin requirement should be? In futures markets, these requirements are set by the clearinghouses. The clearinghouses are what keep the markets and all their transactions running smoothly. In the futures market, especially if people are using brokers, most buyers and sellers are not acquainted with each other, and they are not friends. So who can a futures trader trust, especially when he or she might be buying something and selling it again to complete strangers who may or may not be able to hold up their end of the bargain and meet their financial commitment?

This is where the clearinghouses come in. They promise to back each side (the buyers and sellers) of each trade made

in a futures exchange. The clearinghouse makes sure all of the people involved in futures contracts are doing what they should and fulfilling their agreements. After setting the initial margin requirements, the clearinghouses make sure that

The Chicago Board of Trade is the oldest futures exchange platform in the world. It contains both classic pits for trading futures contracts as well as electronic terminals.

everyone pays the money they should in order to open a contract and all financial obligations are met at the closing out of a contract. The clearinghouse takes no active position in the market, meaning it is not participating in the buying or selling of futures, nor does it represent buyers or sellers. It merely guarantees that the payments associated with a futures contract will be made.

Margin Requirements

At the end of each day, the clearinghouse conducts the daily settlement. The daily settlement, sometimes called marking to market, means updating the margin accounts to show the trading day's gains and losses. This means translating the gains and losses on paper to actual gains and losses that must be paid out to contract holders. The clearinghouse looks at what happened that day and how the prices of commodities changed. Then it settles everyone's accounts. At the end of the day, this could mean the holder of a contract has made money or has lost money.

If the trader lost money, this money comes out of the margin that he or she already put in. Just as the trader had to put the initial margin requirement down to open the contract, he or she must also maintain a certain amount of money in the

Savvy traders can use sites like this one, Quote.com (http://www.quote.com), to monitor the prices of stocks and commodities. Traders can also use them to research factors that might affect prices.

account in order to keep the contract open. This amount is called the maintenance margin requirement. The maintenance margin requirement is less than the initial margin requirement.

If a trader has a really bad day and his or her contract loses a lot of money, the amount of money in the account may fall below the maintenance margin requirement. If that happens, the trader must put more money in the account to bring it back up to the minimum amount of funds required. When a trader must put more money in his or her account, it is known as a margin call. If the value of the contract keeps falling, the trader must keep putting money in the account every day in order to meet the maintenance margin requirement. This additional margin that has to be deposited is called the variation margin.

Another option when stuck with a futures contract that just keeps losing value is to simply close out the position and find another investor to purchase the contract. The trader always has the option to offset his or her position to avoid any more losses.

CALCULATING THE DAILY SETTLEMENT

Determining the daily settlement can be more complicated than it might seem. For one thing, the clearinghouses need a way to determine and calculate the gains and losses. This is complicated by the fact that the prices being set are for future commodities that have not actually been produced, bought, sold, or delivered yet. The prices don't reflect what available commodities are worth today, but what hoped-for commodities might be worth once they do become available. Basically, no actual, physically present commodities are being sold in a futures market.

Because of this, the value or price of a commodity in the futures market is based solely on what people think the commodity will be worth once it is produced, delivered, and ready to go on sale. At this point in time, futures traders are merely speculating (guessing) on the expected supply and demand of a given commodity and its consequent price. They make these guesses based on the best information they have available to them. These information sources can include weather data, crop reports, producer reports, wholesaler's orders, and consumer market research.

To figure out the daily settlement, the clearinghouse takes an average of the last few trades of the day. This tells them what people thought the contracts were worth toward market close. It might seem like it would be simpler to just take the last trade of the day and use that as the settlement price. However, the price of the last trade before the market close might not be representative of the actual price. Since it represents only one transaction, its price could be much higher or lower than those of the other trades earlier in the day. Also, if they knew that the last trade of the day would be used for the settlement price, unscrupulous traders might try to drive up the price of a contract to what they want by overvaluing it in the last trade (or drive the price down by undervaluing a given commodity). By taking an average of the last few transactions, the clearinghouse is able to get a reasonably accurate estimate of what people are paying for each commodity.

MARGINS IN ACTION

The best way to illustrate gains, losses, and the use of margins is with an example. Let's say Linda wants to buy futures contracts in oranges. Now imagine that the cost of orange futures when she wants to buy them is $100. The initial margin requirement is 5 percent. So if Linda wants to open that futures contract, she must deposit $5 in an account to set it up. The maintenance margin requirement is 3 percent. This means that if the amount of money in Linda's account falls below $3, she will have to put more money in.

Linda decides to open the contract in the long position. By taking the long position, Linda is contractually obligated either to buy the oranges or close out (sell) the contract to another buyer before delivery of the oranges. This means that she wants the actual price of oranges to increase by more than the price at which she agreed to buy her oranges. The higher the price of oranges goes, the more money she will make because when she sells either the oranges or the contract, she will receive more money for them than she paid originally.

Now on the first day of trading, imagine that everyone thinks oranges aren't valued very highly. At the end of the day, the price has fallen to $98. This means that Linda loses $2 from her account (which started with $5 in it, the initial margin requirement). So after the first day of trading, Linda has only $3 remaining in her account.

Small changes in the prices of commodities can mean big gains or losses for the holders of futures contracts. Futures traders can monitor their gains and losses electronically.

If on day two, the price fell even further to $97, she would lose another dollar. Now the total in her account would be $2. In order to meet the maintenance margin requirement, Linda would need to deposit another dollar to return her total to $3. Remember that the maintenance margin requirement obligated her to keep at least 3 percent of her $100 investment, or $3, in the account.

On the third day, oranges do better and the settlement price is back up to $102. That's a gain of $5, which, with the $3 already in Linda's account, would bring her total to $8. That might seem like a big gain, but Linda has already put $6 into the account to cover her losses and maintain the margin requirement, so she's really only made $2 in the three days of trading.

PRICE LIMITS

It is certainly possible for a futures contract to make a huge leap in price from day to day. However, in the interest of creating stability and discouraging wild speculation, some futures exchanges impose limits on the price change that can occur from one day to the next. These restrictions are called price limits.

Let's say the price limit was $4 for a given commodity. That means no transaction could take place that created a change of

After the close of trading each day, the trading pit is deserted and littered with discarded paper. The daily settlement has been calculated, and the next day's price limits have been set.

more than $4 in a commodity price in a single day. So with a starting price of $10, the commodity price couldn't go below $6 or above $14. Likewise, the day's settlement price cannot go beyond the price limit. Price limits make it possible for people to accurately predict how much they might win or lose, at least in the short term, by opening a position in a futures contract.

If someone still wants to make a futures transaction that goes above or below the price limit on that contract, the amount will freeze at the limit price. When this happens, the price freeze is called a limit move. In the above example where the limit price was set at $4 and the starting price was $10, let's say a trader wanted to sell a contract for $15. That trade would go beyond the price limit by $1, so the price would remain fixed at $14. If the price is stuck at the upper limit, it is called limit up. If the price is stuck at the lower limit—in this case $6—it is called limit down. Sometimes, the transaction cannot take place at all because it would cause the price to move beyond these upper and lower limits. This situation is called locked limit. It is important to note that not all futures contracts have price limits.

MYTHS and FACTS

MYTH Futures contracts are a kind of stock.

FACT A futures contract is an obligation to buy or sell a commodity at some point in the future at a price agreed upon today. When you buy a stock, you are buying a piece, or share, of a company. You own part of that company. A futures contract does not imply ownership. Instead, it is a promise to buy or sell something in the future.

MYTH There are a limited number of futures contracts available.

FACT Unlike shares of stocks, there is no limit to the supply of futures contracts. Every time a buyer and seller make a trade, a new contract is created.

MYTH In futures contracts, you can only lose as much money as you put down.

FACT In futures trading, the risk is almost unlimited. The holder of a futures contract owes as much money as the value of the contract changed during the period between its signing and the delivery of the commodity.

CHAPTER FOUR
FUTURES IN FLUX

As seen in chapter 3, the potential for change in the value of assets in the futures market is a big part of what makes them a risky investment. But what causes changes in futures contracts and their value? Futures prices are more volatile than stock prices. Buying a company's stock means buying a small piece, or ownership share, of that company. If the company does well, its stock goes up and its investors profit. An established company, known for its long tradition of prudent business practices, popular and reliable products, concern for its investors, and steady profits, will likely continue to prosper. There can be major price swings from time to time, but these kinds of "blue chip" stocks are considered pretty reliable. They generally offer a healthy return on the initial investment over time.

The situation is not so stable in the futures market. A commodity that has performed well one year may collapse the following year. The futures trader can simply never sit back and wait for the money to come in. A lot of work is required to figure out how the price of a given commodity might change in the near future and why it will do so.

When students have to write reports for school, they research their topic by delving into a number of sources, sorting out the information, and drawing conclusions about what seems like the reasonable truth. Traders have to do the same in order to keep up-to-date on the rapidly changing futures market.

Traders rely on a number of resources to research what they think will happen in the futures market. Good futures traders don't just look at what is happening now, they must also try to anticipate what will happen in the days, weeks, and months ahead. Today's prices may have already taken into account tomorrow's conditions. Also, it is important to remember that no one factor controls these conditions. Everything from bad weather, labor strikes, and transportation problems, to political volatility and increased demand in developing nations can affect the supply, delivery, and price of a given commodity.

What Causes Prices to Change?

Weather is a major concern for many agricultural commodities. No one can control the weather. It can be difficult to predict and can change quickly from day to day. Oranges growing in Florida need a lot of sunshine to prosper. Wheat and corn in the fields of the Midwest need the right balance of rain and sunshine. While meteorologists can predict what will happen in the coming week, they can't accurately predict what will

Unavoidable and difficult-to-predict weather conditions like extreme drought can cause devastation to crops. This reduction of the quantity of the crop available will make the price of the commodity increase.

happen in the coming year. In addition to normal weather variables like the amount of rain or the temperature outside, there is also the possibility of natural disasters. A hurricane, tsunami, or severe drought could wreak havoc on an area and wipe out

an entire year's crop in a matter of hours or days.

Many other factors can affect the price of a commodity. Changes in government of the country where the commodity is grown, mined, or raised can cause changes in the amount produced. If a war breaks out in a nation that produces a lot of bananas, it will affect the number of bananas produced that year. If a new government takes power, or if the old government enforces new regulations on how the commodity is produced, the amount of the commodity that year may also be impacted.

The supply of a commodity affects how much it will sell for, but so does the demand for it. Usually, the higher the supply of a commodity, the lower the price. Where there is high demand, however, prices will usually rise. Supply is easy to quantify, but demand is not. Demand is about what people are willing and able to buy. The question to ask when determining demand is: How badly do consumers want this commodity or the products it can make, and can they afford it? The demand for a commodity depends

The frequently changing price of crude oil, from which gasoline is refined, is due in part to what futures speculators think will happen. Higher crude oil prices result in higher prices at the pump for gasoline.

in part on the price at which it is being offered. Demand for some commodities, like in the energy market, may not respond much to price increases. People always need energy to power their homes and drive their cars. Because energy is a necessity, people will pay what they have to in order to get it. However, demand for other products, such as feed grains for livestock, may be more sensitive to price increases because of the availability of alternative substitutes. If the price of one feed grain goes too high, farmers could buy less expensive grain to feed their livestock.

The difficulty of knowing what the demand will be for a commodity is one of the trickiest points to consider with futures contracts. Traders rely on a number of sources to predict what the supply and demand of a given commodity will be. A lot of this information can come from the U.S. government. Government organizations like the U.S. Department of Agriculture (USDA) release reports with a lot of helpful information to traders of agricultural commodities. This information includes estimates of the number of hogs by weight category, the number of acres of specific crops planted by farmers, monthly updates of crop production estimates, and much more. All of this information is available free to the public. Many traders spend a lot of time examining figures to try to identify trends in the market before they happen.

FINANCIAL FUTURES' RELATIONSHIP TO THE OVERALL ECONOMY

Financial futures are affected most by the overall health of the economy. Everything from the stock market to the value of currency can be traced back to how people feel about the economy and its future. If consumer confidence in the economy is high, people tend to spend money in stores. Companies make larger profits. Industrial output and employment increase. And more and more money begins circulating throughout the entire economy. If consumer confidence is low and spending drops, the economy becomes cash-starved, production slows, and jobs are lost. Futures traders may then predict reduced demand for many types of nonessential commodities.

Keeping an Eye on the Sky

Even in our advanced society, we still live at the mercy of the weather. The weather has an impact on a number of industries, such as agriculture, energy, entertainment, construction, and travel, among many others. Since the weather affects so many aspects of the economy, it's no wonder that people eventually started trading futures contracts on the weather itself.

The contract for a weather-based future looks just like that of a commodity- or finance-based future. Instead of promising to buy or sell something, the holder of the contract is sort of promising a specific type of weather. The fluctuations (movement up or down) in price are based upon changes in weather, rather than changes in value. For example, a trader can purchase a contract for how much snow he or she thinks will fall. This contract might say that 1 inch (2.5 centimeters) of snow is equal to $200. Then every time the amount of actual snowfall changes by $\frac{1}{10}$ of an inch (0.25 cm), the contract value would change by $20.

In order to predict the changes to financial futures, traders look at a number of economic indicators. First, they might consider the gross domestic product (GDP), which is a measure of all economic activity within a country. They might also look at the unemployment rate and the number of houses people are buying. Falling unemployment rates and more people buying houses can mean increased confidence in the economy. As with a lot of the resources that traders of commodity futures consult and analyze, most of this information is available for free online from the federal government.

Technical Analysis

While many futures traders keep track of all the possible factors that may affect price changes to a commodity, others follow a system called technical trading. Technical trading is the belief that all the information that causes prices to change will show up in a price movement that can be charted. Rather than look at individual factors like political events, planting data, weather, or natural disasters, traders will make charts. In making these charts, the traders hope to analyze short- and long-term price patterns in the market. If their analysis is correct, they can accurately anticipate when periods of rising or falling prices will occur and quickly profit from the price fluctuations (movement up or down) without necessarily knowing the specific reasons for them.

Bar charts are one of the more popular tools for traders. They can include information on a particular futures market's price movements. Such charts can be designed to reveal the price fluctuations of a commodity on a daily, weekly, and monthly basis.

Because many traders are interested in taking a technical analysis approach to futures trading, there are many Web sites devoted to making and displaying charts that some traders might find helpful, like this one found at www.barchart.com.

Studying historical patterns can help provide a long-term perspective on the market. With the help of computers, the traders can easily spot price trends.

Charting is not an exact science, however. Allowance must be made for errors and anomalies (onetime variations from the norm), and unexpected events can disrupt forecasts made on chart patterns. Whether traders choose to research the specific events that make prices change or just chart the results of those changes, they will never be able to perfectly predict what the futures market will do.

CHAPTER FIVE
FLUCTUATING FUTURES PRICES AND THE AVERAGE CONSUMER

In the futures market, prices tend to fluctuate and adjust quickly due to changes in the world. The futures market is actually a very good indicator of how the stock market and economy in general are doing because changes in the futures market are usually seen first. This is because the investors in the futures market are constantly keeping track of important and relevant developments. These include the weather, government policy and leadership, stock indexes, and other important indicators that might have a bearing on the commodities or financial futures they are invested in.

If someone starts to notice a futures contract is undervalued or overvalued, he or she will immediately try to use that knowledge to gain a profit. Arbitrageurs are people who constantly watch the relationship between cash and futures contracts to spot any possible mispricing. If, for example, an arbitrageur saw that corn futures in a certain month were overpriced compared to the actual cash value of corn, the arbitrageur would immediately sell those contracts. The arbitrageur could make an easy profit. However, these opportunities don't last long. Traders on the floor of the exchange would start to notice the heavy selling activity and react by pushing down the price of corn futures. This would bring the price of corn futures back in line with their real value. The futures market is constantly changing and righting itself to stay in line with the cash market (the actual price that people are willing to pay for a commodity).

Price Discovery

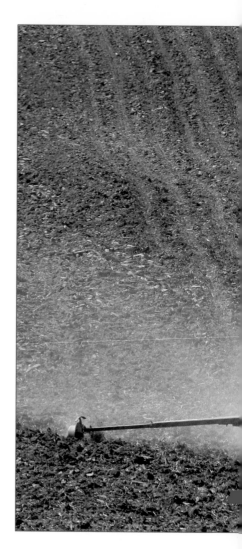

Yet this can work in the opposite direction, too. The futures market can sometimes predict and change prices in the cash market before they happen. This process is called price discovery. Price discovery is the process of determining what the price of a commodity will be in the future through the interactions of buyers and sellers today. The process of price discovery helps reveal information about future cash market prices through the futures market.

Price discovery can be very useful for farmers, miners, and other producers of commodities.

Let's say the owner of a silver mine that hasn't produced much silver in the past is trying to figure out if it's worth keeping the mine open. Unless he or she can get a good price for the small amount of silver the mine will produce, the cost of mining it

Farmers have to make decisions about what to plant long before the harvest. This farmer is planting corn because of the increasingly profitable ethanol fuel that can be made from corn.

will be too high to make a decent profit. It takes a long time to mine silver and get it ready for market, but the owner needs to decide about opening the mine right now.

To make a decision, the owner doesn't need to know the price that silver is going for now, but what the price will be in a year when the silver will be ready to sell. While the owner can't know for certain what the price of silver will be next year, he or she can get a good estimate using the futures market. The price given for a silver futures contract that expires in one year is a useful estimate of the commodity's future price. If that number is high enough, the owner would decide to keep the mine open. If the number is very low, the owner might decide to halt mining operations for at least a year until silver prices rebound again.

As seen in the previous chapter, factors such as weather or political upheaval can create day-to-day price changes in the futures market. However, through price discovery, sometimes the biggest changes don't come from actual events or conditions, but simply what people think will happen. In many ways, what people think the value of a given commodity will be in the near future is what determines its actual value.

Both gold and oil are important commodities whose futures contracts values fluctuate a great deal. By looking at what causes major price changes in these futures contracts, we can get a better general understanding of how the overall economy impacts futures markets and ordinary consumers.

GOLD

Gold is a precious metal used throughout the world. People use gold in jewelry and electronics. Gold is also used as a way to store monetary value securely, as in gold bars and coins. Although paper currency may fluctuate wildly in value and even become worthless during periods of hyperinflation, gold will always remain a precious metal, valuable in itself.

For this reason, people tend to believe in the enduring value of gold, even during economic crises. The metal is considered a good protection against economical or political uncertainties. Many central banks back their currency using gold reserves. This means that the paper currency actually represents a certain value in gold. Currency holders can, in theory at least, go to a bank and exchange their paper money for the equivalent amount of gold.

The United States is the world's second largest producer of gold. There are some special characteristics of this commodity that make its futures contracts very different from those of other commodities. Because gold can be stored forever and is not affected by weather conditions, its supply is not subject to wide swings year to year. Actually, the stock of gold held in reserve is much larger than the annual production of newly mined gold. The supply of gold has a smaller impact on its demand than many other factors do. Gold prices are most sensitive to political and economic factors. When people have less faith in the value of their currency, the demand for gold increases.

Gold futures shot up in value as the recession took hold in the United States in 2008. A recession is a period of economic downturn. The price of gold went up because people believe in the ongoing value of gold and demand more of it, especially when the value of their paper money begins to erode. With the U.S. dollar losing value during the recession, people didn't want to keep their money strictly in currency.

The demand for gold increases during recessions because people feel it's a safe investment during hard times, when the value of currency typically falls.

As people gain more faith in the dollar, the price of gold futures tends to go down. For this reason, futures prices in gold are an excellent indicator of the health of the economy. The changing prices of gold show just how much confidence people

have in their currency and their economy. When gold prices rise, it can be taken as a sign of economic weakness and consumer unease. When gold prices fall, it can be taken as a sign of a return to economic robustness and consumer confidence.

OIL

Oil futures behave differently from many other commodity-based futures. Normally, in order for the price of a commodity-based future to go up, there must be a low supply and a high demand. However, oil futures don't always behave this way. In 2010, there were ample supplies of both oil and unleaded gasoline in the United States. Because the supply was relatively high, the price of unleaded gasoline fell somewhat. Weak demand during the recession also drove prices down. This makes sense under the normal rules of supply and demand. However, at the same time that the price of unleaded gasoline went down, the price of crude oil (from which gasoline is refined) had actually gone up. This is a unique quality of the oil futures market that needs to be examined further.

This semisubmersible oil platform in the Gulf of Mexico was damaged in July 2005 following a hurricane. The sinking led to speculation that there would be oil shortages in the near future.

The global supply of oil is largely controlled by an international cartel called the Organization of Petroleum Exporting Countries (OPEC). OPEC is an organization of twelve oil-producing countries that produce 46 percent of the world's oil.

In 1960, these twelve nations formed an alliance to regulate the supply, and therefore the price, of oil worldwide. These countries realized that oil was a limited, nonrenewable, but essential resource. If each of the twelve nations competed with the others to sell its oil to non-oil-producing nations, the price of oil would sink very low, as each nation tried to under-cut the other to gain customers. In the end, all twelve nations would lose money if they engaged in open competition.

Instead, the twelve nations decided to band together to set production limits and fix prices, ensuring that each OPEC country would sell its oil at the agreed-upon price and all member nations would earn higher profits. The goal of OPEC in the late 2000s was to keep the price of oil at around $70 per barrel. If the price rose much higher, other non-OPEC countries would have incentives to drill new oil fields, which is too expensive a proposition when global oil prices are low.

The United States stores seven hundred million barrels of oil in reserve. These reserves can be used to increase the domestic supply of oil when necessary. The reserves come in handy during times when demand for oil is much higher than the supply, resulting in skyrocketing prices. This can happen because of natural disasters, such as hurricanes, which can damage offshore oil rigs in water. Supply problems can also occur during times of war in the Middle East (where most of the OPEC nations are located). This can also happen when OPEC is in the midst of a political dispute with the United States and other Western nations and seeks to choke off vital oil supplies in retribution.

Traders in oil futures bid on the price of oil based on what they think oil will trade at a certain future date. They look at projected supply and demand to determine the price. If traders think the price of oil will increase in the future, they bid up the price of oil. However, this can become a self-fulfilling prophecy. By thinking that the price of oil will go up, the traders often end up making the actual price of oil go up. This can create high oil prices, even during times of ample supply.

Once this upward push starts, other investors will bid on oil prices just like any other commodity and create a bubble of ever-increasing prices. This price bubble often goes on to directly impact the consumer. Traders who bring the price of oil up often bring the price of gas up, too. This can be frustrating when high prices at the pump seem to indicate a lack of supply that doesn't in fact exist.

Effects on the Consumer

The trading of oil futures and resulting price fluctuations are not the only commodity futures trading that strongly affects ordinary consumers. Futures often directly affect consumer

REDEEM POINTS FOR
OROWEAT TEAM USA GEAR!

GEAR UP
FOR THE
GOLD!
2008 BEIJING

OROWEAT.

Country

100% WHOLE WHEAT

Grams   No Trans Fat   Heart Healthy

E101
ENTENMANNS/OROWEAT

REGULAR PRICE
/1 /24 OZ $4.69

539

Special

OROWEAT 100%

Consumers feel the effects of futures trading of commodities in their every-day lives. The price of this loaf of bread is directly affected by the price of the wheat that was used to make it. Wheat's commodity price is influenced, in turn, by speculators' buying and selling of wheat futures contracts.

YOU SAVE: $1.20
0-73130-03701   08/18/08
08/31/08

AZZA'S
E FOODS
ally Growing

prices. If the price of a commodity goes up, it means that all the goods made from that commodity will increase in price, too. If futures contracts for wheat go up, for example, so will the price of bread and cereal made from that wheat. If the futures price of cotton goes up, so will the price of the clothes we buy. By estimating what they think the price for commodities will be in the future, traders often end up affecting how much ordinary people pay for the goods they need in their everyday life.

So the next time you buy a juicy tomato or a dozen eggs, you can think about all the people involved in setting the price for these products. When you buy a commodity, or a product made from a commodity, you are seeing firsthand the far-reaching effects of the futures market on the overall economy, your domestic economy, and on your daily life.

Ten Great Questions
to Ask a Financial Adviser

1 How much money do I need to put down in order to open this futures contract?

2 How much money might I lose in this investment, and how much cash should I keep on hand to cover any losses?

3 Are there any daily price limits on this futures contract?

4 How can I accurately predict which futures contracts will do well and whether the price will go up or down?

5 Where can I research information on the specific commodity for which I wish to open a futures contract?

6 Are some futures markets more reliable than others?

7 Which is a better investment for me: commodity-based futures or financial futures? Which is safer? Which offers a better return on investment?

8 If I get a margin call, should I put more money in the account or just close out (trade) the contract?

9 How do futures prices affect me as a consumer of goods and commodities?

10 Are there any futures I can trust to remain stable from year to year?

GLOSSARY

arbitrageur A traders in the futures market who looks for undervalued contracts to make a quick profit from.

clearinghouse An organization that guarantees all trades in the futures market.

close out To no longer have a futures contract; to trade or sell it off.

commodity A raw, unprocessed good.

currency future A futures contract based on the change in the value of money.

daily settlement At the end of the day, deciding a commodity's starting price for the next day.

futures contract An agreement to buy or sell a certain commodity, at a certain time in the future, to be delivered to a certain place.

futures exchange A place where people can trade futures contracts; sometimes called a trading exchange.

hedger A person who trades futures contracts based on commodities he or she has a business interest in.

initial margin requirement The amount of money a trader must put down to open a futures contract.

limit down When the price of a futures contract freezes at the lower limit.

limit move What happens when the price freezes at one of the price limits.

limit up When the price of a futures contract freezes at the upper limit.

locked limit When a transaction cannot be made because it would push the price of a futures contract over or under the price limit.

long position The buyer in a futures contract.

maintenance margin requirement The amount of money a trader must keep in his or her account to hold a futures contract.

margin In the futures market, the money a trader must put down to hold a contract.

margin call In the futures market, when a trader must put down more margin in order to keep a futures contract.

offset To close a futures account by buying a contract equal to the value of one you have sold, or selling one equal to the value of one you have bought.

price discovery The process of determining what the price of a commodity will be in the future through the interactions of buyers and sellers today.

price limit A restriction on the amount the price of a futures contract can change in a single day.

short position The seller in a futures contract.

speculator A person who trades futures contracts in commodities he or she doesn't have an actual business interest in.

trading exchange A place where people can trade futures contracts; sometimes called a futures exchange.

variation margin The extra margin that has to be deposited after a margin call.

FOR MORE INFORMATION

American Association of Individual Investors (AAII)
625 North Michigan Avenue
Chicago, IL 60611
(800) 428-2244
Web site: http://www.aaii.com
The AAII is a nonprofit organization that provides individual
investors with resources and educational tools to succeed
in financial planning. It offers helpful information about
getting started in futures trading.

CME Group
20 South Wacker Drive
Chicago, IL 60606
(312) 930-1000
Web site: http://www.cmegroup.com
The CME Group is the world's largest and most diverse
marketplace for derivatives, including futures. The group
controls the Chicago Board of Trade (CBOT), which
first created futures contracts.

ICE Futures Canada
400 Commodity Exchange Tower
360 Main Street

Winnipeg, MB R3C 3Z4
Canada
(204) 925-5000
Web site: https://www.theice.com/futures_canada.jhtml
Established in 1887, ICE Futures Canada is Canada's leading
    agricultural exchange and was the first fully electronic
    exchange in North America.

MF Global
123 Front Street West, Suite 1601
Toronto, ON M5J 2M2
Canada
(416)-862-7000
Web site: http://www.mfglobal.ca
MF Global is a leading brokerage firm servicing the Canadian
    futures and options markets.

National Futures Association (NFA)
300 South Riverside Plaza, #1800
Chicago, IL 60606-6615
(312) 781-1300
Web site: http://www.nfa.futures.org
The NFA is a self-regulatory organization for the U.S. futures
    industry. It is an independent organization with no ties
    to any market.

U.S. Commodity Futures Trading Commission (CFTC)
Three Lafayette Centre
1155 21st Street NW
Washington, DC 20581

(202) 418-5000

Web site: http://www.cftc.gov

The CFTC is a U.S. government commission made up of
 five commissioners appointed by the president. The
 commission monitors futures markets and market
 participants closely.

WEB SITES

Due to the changing nature of Internet links, Rosen Publishing
has developed an online list of Web sites related to the subject
of this book. This site is updated regularly. Please use this link
to access the list:

http://www.rosenlinks.com/rwe/hfw

FOR FURTHER READING

Alexander, Colin. *Timing Techniques for Commodity Futures Markets: Effective Strategy and Tactics for Short-Term and Long-Term Traders*. New York, NY: McGraw-Hill, 2007.

Bennie, Paul. *The Great Chicago Fire of 1871* (Great Historic Disasters). New York, NY: Chelsea House Publications, 2008.

Chicago Board of Trade. *The Chicago Board of Trade Handbook of Futures and Options*. New York, NY: McGraw-Hill, 2006.

Furgang, Kathy. *How the Stock Market Works* (Real World Economics). New York, NY: Rosen Publishing, 2010.

Hart, Joyce. *How Inflation Works* (Real World Economics). New York, NY: Rosen Publishing, 2009.

Holihan, Mary B. *The Complete Guide to Investing in Commodity Trading & Futures: How to Earn High Rates of Returns Safely*. Ocala, FL: Atlantic Publishing Group, 2008.

Hollander, Barbara Gottfried. *How Currency Devaluation Works* (Real World Economics). New York, NY: Rosen Publishing, 2011.

Jankovsy, Jason Alan. *The Art of the Trade: What I Learned (and Lost) Trading the Chicago Futures Markets*. Hoboken, NJ: Wiley, 2008.

Kallen, Stuart A. *The Gas Crisis* (Ripped from the Headlines). Yankton, SD: Erickson Press, 2007.

Katz, John. *The Goldwatcher: Demystifying Gold Investing.* Hoboken, NJ: Wiley, 2008.

La Bella, Laura. *How Commodities Trading Works* (Real World Economics). New York, NY: Rosen Publishing, 2011.

Nagle, Jeanne. *How a Recession Works* (Real World Economics). New York, NY: Rosen Publishing, 2009.

Schnepf, Randy. *High Agricultural Commodity Prices: What Are the Issues?*. New York, NY: Nova Science Publishers, 2008.

BIBLIOGRAPHY

Bhar, Ramaprasad, and Shigeyuki Hamori. "Information Flow Between Price Changes and Trading Volume in Gold Futures Contracts." *International Journal of Business and Economics*, 2004, Vol 3, No. 1, pg 45–56.

Chance, Don M. "Futures Market and Contracts." *Derivatives and Alternative Investments*. Boston, MA: Pearson Custom Publishing, 2009.

Holihan, Mary B. *The Complete Guide to Investing in Commodity Trading & Futures: How to Earn High Rates of Returns Safely*. Ocala, FL: Atlantic Publishing Group, 2008.

Jankovsy, Jason Alan. *The Art of the Trade: What I Learned (and Lost) Trading the Chicago Futures Markets*. Hoboken, NJ: Wiley, 2008.

Kolb, Robert W., and James A. Overdahl. *Futures, Options, and Swaps*. 5th ed. New York, NY: Blackwell Publishing, 2007.

Marthinsen, John. *Risk Takers: Uses and Abuses of Financial Derivatives*. 2nd ed. New York, NY: Pearson Education, Inc., 2009.

Ray, Tiernan. "IEA Raises Oil Forecast, But Futures, Oil Stocks Dip." *Barron's*, February 11, 2010. Retrieved March 2010 (http://blogs.barrons.com/

stockstowatchtoday/2010/02/11/iea-raises-oil-forecast-but-futures-oil-stocks-dip).

Sykora, Allen. "Precious Metals: NY Gold Suffers from Renewed Risk Aversion." *Dow Jones Newswires*, January 28, 2010. Retrieved March 2010 (http://online.wsj.com/article/BT-CO-20100126-707692.html?mod=WSJ_latestheadlines).

U.S. Commodity Futures Trading Commission. "Future Market Basics." December 19, 2009. Retrieved March 2010 (http://www.cftc.gov/educationcenter/futuresmarketbasics.html).

Walcoff, Matt. "Canada Stocks Rise as Oil, Gold Rally on Weaker U.S. Dollar." *Business Week*, February 16, 2010. Retrieved March 2010 (http://www.businessweek.com/news/2010-02-16/canada-stocks-rise-as-oil-gold-rally-on-weaker-u-s-dollar.html).

INDEX

About the Author

Susan Meyer is a writer working in the children's educational publishing market. Meyer is a frequent user of commodities in her everyday life. She is often confounded by the high price of bread and cereal, despite her understanding of wheat and grain futures. Meyer lives in Queens, New York.

Photo Credits

Cover (top) © www.istockphoto.com/Lilli Day; cover (bottom), pp. 12–13 Scott Olson/Getty Images; pp. 1 (left), 3, 4–5 © www.istockphoto.com/Dean Turner; p. 6 Robert Sullivan/AFP/ Getty Images; pp. 8, 21, 33, 46, 55 Mario Tama/Getty Images; p. 9 © North Wind/North Wind Picture Archives; pp. 14–15 Andre Harrer/Bloomberg/ Getty Images; pp. 18–19 Daniel Acker/Bloomberg via Getty Images; pp. 22–23 David Aubrey/Taxi/Getty Images; pp. 24–25, 42–43 The CME Group, A CME/Chicago Board of Trade/NYMEX Company; pp. 28–29 Stockbyte/ Thinkstock; pp. 30–31, 40–41, 50, 60–61 Shutterstock; pp. 34–35 Frank Polich/Bloomberg via Getty Images; pp. 36–37 www.Quote.com; pp. 48–49 Lowell Georgia/ National Geographic/Getty Images; p. 54 Courtesy of Barchart.com; pp. 56–57 Mark Hirsch/Getty Images; pp. 62–63, 65 © AP Images; pp. 68, 70, 73, 75, 77 © www. istockphoto.com/studiovision.

Designer: Sam Zavieh; Photo Researcher: Marty Levick